SHATTERED

AND

SCATTERED

A RANDOM POETIC TRIP

© 2011 Manuel Nava Leal

ISBN: 9780983486879

Creative House International Press, Inc.
CreativeHousePress.com

This book is dedicated to my children; Pedro, Genaro, Gina and to my wife Ana Isabel, as well as to all lovers of poetry. May all of you find peace, happiness and joy in this small collection of poetry that you might share with those you love.

Table of Contents

Table of Contents (Cont.)

Table of Contents (Cont.)

Table of Contents (Cont.)

A Humble Bath

The rain finally ends
Leaving its presence behind
Saturated plants
Smile broadly at the mighty sun
Quenched at last
Turning my head as I drive
A lonely Houston back road
My eyes widen in surprise
I see a Hispanic male
Bathing in a muddy puddle
Using a plastic container
As a filthy scoop
Rinsing the lather away
Sullied water cascades
Past protruding ribs
I slow to view
Insanity…
Grease stained elbows
Raised head high
Eyes closed in ecstasy
Lips muttering silently they
Smile broadly at the mighty sun
He sits cross legged
Looking like a
Drenched Hindi God
Bare knees make waves
Playfully bouncing in joy
He suddenly stands
Revealing dark stained
Once-whitey tidies
I quickly look away
In embarrassment
He howls loudly like a wolf
As I drive off
Shaking my head

I can only
Smile broadly at the mighty sun
A humble bath
Forever soaked into my psyche

A Man's Prayer

Lord, teach me to accept and help me to endure
The hurts that pain me, physically and emotionally
Restrain me Oh Lord, from wounding those around me
Especially, those I love

Lord, remind me that I was once a little boy
And am, still a child at heart to this very day.
Prompt me Oh Lord, to use the child within
To enjoy life and share that joy with others.

Adios Harlingen

My older sisters and I sat crossed legged,
our backs to the rear door and window of the green and white station
  Wagon.
My uncle's vehicle was huge and fully loaded with our possessions.
Uncle Fidias, Aunt Rosario, Cousin Sergio and the seven of us ready
  to go
*Looking back years later, we've wondered what life would have been
  like had we stayed.*

Our parents had divorced on my thirteenth birthday.
Before us was the beginning of a frightening voyage,
into an unknown future in a large city called, Houston.
We sat in silence as we drove away from our house.
*Today, I half jokingly say that I got a divorce for a birthday present
that year.*

Halfway down the block we began to reminisce about our lives in our
  tiny town.
The three of us turned around facing the rear window,
aware without saying, that this was the end of a way of life,
Arturo, Ruben and Yolanda our brothers and sister were too young to
  understand
Harlingen had been our world it had meant everything to us.

Look! Lupe said, "There's the house where Manuel lifted that boy by
  the collar!"
"That kid shot Rosalinda on the back with a BB gun, remember?"
"There's Juanita's house, where we ate oatmeal for the first time!"
Adios Juanita!
"And there's Jaime's place." "He found the ten-dollar bill Manuel lost
  and gave it back!"
*My mother had sent me to buy bread for Dad's lunch and I had
  dropped it.*

"Smell that?" "Bread baking at the Rainbo Bakery!" "Adios, sweet
  aroma!"
"Remember the giant Christmas displays, and the tours of the plant?"
"They'd hand out cookies and those tiny loaves of bread!"
"Hey, don't forget the Christmas parades downtown, and "Las Posa
  das," at church!"
*We didn't have much growing up in that small town, but it seemed we
  didn't need much.*

"Look!" "Look!" "There's the building with the Pepsi sign on the side!"
"Bye, bye!"
"That's where carnivals were held!" "Yeah, every year!" "Bye, bye!"
"Daddy took us to Serena, "The Human Seal," at the freak show."
"She had no arms, just the tiniest hands, I shook one, it was so soft,
  remember?"
*Carnivals made me aware that the world had so many strange yet
  wonderful people.*

"There's the canning plant where Daddy works." "Bye plant!" "Adios,
  Daddy."
"Remember the dances they held in the parking lot, right over there,
  up front?"
"Oh, remember the ramp where trucks unloaded fruit to the con
  veyor?"
"We could go in there and take whatever didn't make it on the con
  veyor!"
*Dad had been a supervisor there for nineteen years. He was laid-off
  just before retirement.*

"Mira, El Grande Theater they show Mexican movies there!" "Haven't
  gone in a while."
"There's Sears, where Rosalinda won a poster contest once!" "First
  prize!" "Adios!"
"There's the cantina where Daddy and I split a beer." "Well, not really,
  I took two sips."
"I saw Daddy beat a guy at billiards there, the man was *so* mad but
  Daddy just smiled."

9

Our Fathers' car was always parked in front of a cantina when he wasn't at work.

"That's the way to Gay Junior High and Vernon High School." "Bye, bye!"
"Manuel was so nervous, he'd throw-up the first day of school every year, remember?"
"Lupe, remember the fries and ketchup at the place across from school?" "You took us!"
"Hey look, there's the cotton-mill!" "Remember picking cotton in sum mer?"
Today, the scent of boiling cottonseed oil brings with it a mix of emo tions.

After reaching the old highway, we turned around.
The three of us stared ahead with blank expressions, falling silent
"Adios, Harlingen." "Adios, childhood."
"Adios."
I felt like throwing up.

Adult Talk

Stupid!
Me?
Shut up!
Why?
Mind your own business!
But, I'm curious
Smart ass!
Smart ass?
Go away!
And go where?
This is adult talk!
Gossiping?
Act your age!
You're not
Get me a beer!
I want a sip
Go play with your friends!
I don't have any

Ancient Ways

Theology has thousands of faces
Lack of faith brings consequences
Rituals were once a practiced dance
We tearfully beg for one more chance
Quietly genuflecting on bent knee
Feverishly fingering prayer beads
Evangelists praise the Lord on TV sets
Who, fly round the globe in private jets
Rebirth seen in Nature's way
Doctors manipulating DNA
Cemeteries slowly disappear
Holding remains in urns so dear
Where candles once quietly burned
Neon lights brightly mourn
Scientists rapidly unlock mysteries
Ancient ways have become ancient history

And The World Goes On

At road's end
Nothing is before us
That we haven't
Seen, touched,
Tasted, known
Nowhere else to go
Nothing left
To experience anew
The road ends here
And the world goes on
Without you
Physical being ceases
An abrupt finality
Death is the beginning
Of something new
A journey through chaos
Return if you wish
As what or whom,
Who knows?
No regrets if not
And the world goes on
With or without you
Not once caring
One way or another
As you're forever now
A part of the whole

Another Day

The sun slowly rolled over and awoke
Tired and sore
And decided to pull the clouds over itself like blankets
Making an effort to sleep once more

The clouds however, full of thunderous rage
Flashed lightning furiously and rumbled as if to say
"How dare you, use us so callously!"
So, they shook the sun mightily until he rose to start another day

Astral Shore

Vibrant pulsing stars
Inflame my soul and heart
While flinging sparks
Like massive fiery darts

Tyrian purple is no more
As light through darkness bore
Exposing stars to adore
Splayed out on surging astral shore

Beyond

Beyond the Milky Way
Past stars unnamed
Exceeding the deepest space
Rush our echoes into the void

Beyond undiscovered universes
Past infinite light
Exceeding the barren dark
Hasten our reflections into the void

Beyond countless suns
Past our finite lives
Exceeding the here and now
Dash our dreams into the void

Bitter Times

Bitter times and the living ain't easy
Cold showers pour, freezing my soul
Sharp words sting swelling my brains
Thoughts are stiff, stunted without reason
Heart feels heavy, as heavy as stone
Smiles are few and laughter to painful to bear
Dark clouds hover and cover the sun
Brightest light as illusive as the stars
Ground is frozen, grass is frost bitten
Bitter times and a tempest is blowing
Dogs are barking and none are fenced in
Storm is coming and shelter is down
No prior warning, the enemy at the door
Foundation is crumbling
And there's no where to run
Bitter times and the living ain't easy

Blades of Grass

Warm winds blow
Over silent pastures
Stirring blades of grass
In lonely, empty fields
Waves rise and fall
And would be lifting spirits
If anyone were there
Blades of grass
Swirl ever so gently
Only the dead can hear
The quiet winds
Mounds of grass
Catch sunlight
As they rise and fall
Breathing the air
Caressing each blade
With gentle gales
Gliding in from
Who knows where?

Book of Life

A table of contents
Guides us to the massacre
A list of bloodied and guilt ridden
Souls of a world gone awry

An appendix referencing
Martyrs and saints
Who walked on this earth
Skin sacks heavy with sin

Truth
Is always a victim of books
Like the proverbial lamb led to slaughter
Bloodletting on the pages of life

Lest we forget
We are the consequence
Paragraphs that fill chapter and verse
Which lead to the inevitable End

Bubbles

Life is not a circle as popularly believed
It is a lather of vibrant rainbow bubbles
Holding fast to one another
Sporadically bursting here and there
In a vibrant chain reaction
Delivering energy affecting all
Exploding memories and ideas
Touching friend and foe
Experiencing song and sadness
Nurturing love and pain
Our lives are vibrant rainbow bubbles
Souls and suds holding on for dear life
Exploding here and there
In a vibrant chain reaction of energy
Affecting one and all

Butterfly Laugh

Butterflies surround me
Glittery wings shimmer sunlight
One lands on me
Lightly tasting my nose
She pushed herself off
And fluttering away
I heard her laugh
Astonished and perplexed
I couldn't help but join her
We laughed merrily
At the silliness of it all
"What made you laugh?
I asked
"What do you find so funny?"
Her response
Was to flitter about happily
She did not laugh aloud again
But she bounced through the air
With such beguiling joy
I found her quite humorous
"What did she find so amusing in me?"
"Was I sweet or salty?"
I chuckled to myself
Yet, I closed my eyes
Concentrating
I began to wonder
"Would I hear her once more?"
I began to ponder
"Do insects laugh?"
"Can they?"
"What would they find so delightful?"
"Themselves?"
"Each other?"
"Humans?"
"Have you ever heard an insect laugh?"

I'd never considered such things
"Did I actually hear a butterfly laugh?"
"If not, does it matter now?"
But, I wonder still

Butterfly Wings

Images of butterfly wings
Flutter in my thoughts
Bright sunlight
Reflecting
Intricate patterns
While diminutive scales
Swirl downward like
Multi-colored snowflakes
Which delicately land
On my face

Cantina Life

Slouching on an old rickety wooden chair
Staring at a girl and not too subtle
Sweet tanned skin. long black silky hair
Can't seem to find happiness in this bottle

An hombre cries out, his prideful Mexican joy
Listening to the jukebox play a Corrida
You're on the wrong side of the border, boy!
But we're all just drunks in this old cantina

It's hot enough to melt the blues
The Señorita softly singing takes my hand
Pulls me to her as she kicks off her shoes
I pull back and gently guide her to my lap

Since these cold beers don't offer much relief
I'll take this girl/woman's hot lovemaking
Rather lose myself in her heat
As we walk to my truck I feel her body shaking

Captain

Monstrous waves roil and churn the seas about me
Battering my tiny ship upon the terrible salty brine
The tempest blows mightily
Knocking me off balance many times over
I lash myself to the mast
My head beating furiously against it
No relief, no respite
And why should there be?
I helped create the hurricane
The author of my own fate
Captain of my own shit

Cemetery Stroll

Sun reflects from
Bleached and polished
Marble, granite tombstones
A wintry breeze skims
Over and around their surface
Numbing my bones
Stabbing like a frozen dagger
Stopping my pulse momentarily
Lips dry and cracked
Refuse to move
My throat as tight
As a Hercules knot
Refusing to release a sound
The pain of silence
Serves to remind
Of muted voices
Beneath my gliding shadow
I muffle a throaty cough
Not wishing to startle
The perpetually at rest
I came to speak to them
The dead
No, I came to address them
To visit if only for a while
No one else is here
"Hello everyone," I begin
"We miss you."
"We long for your wisdom and counsel."
"Do you dream of us?"
"Are you in good company?"
"Do you wish to be heard?"
"What secrets did you take with you?"
"Did you fear revealing them?"
"Were you embarrassed, or ashamed?"
"Would they have caused harm?"

"Were they so terrible?"
"So frightening?"
"I want to know your secrets."
"I need to know."
"Today is All Saint's Day."
"Where are your families?"
"Why are they not here?"
"You only have me here, a stranger."
"It may seem you are forgotten."
"I guarantee you are not."
It is early still
The ground is covered in mist
Others will soon follow
With flowers and tears
Some will remember and laugh
Some will sit still
Preferring silence, perhaps prayer
"Memories of you linger,
in the hearts and minds
of those you touched."
"It may seem that most
have no time for the dead."
"But it is fear that keeps them away."
"As though you'd contaminate them with death."
"Why I wonder?"
As I wander past many tombs
"Why do we fear accompanying you?"
"After all, we have no choice."
"We will all arrive soon enough, I suppose"
"We too will rest in darkness beneath the sun."
I read names, dates and epitaphs
Some make me smile,
And for the children I weep
Tiny hands no longer held
Small warm bodies we'll never again hold
Those touch me deeply
"You wise ones knew so much and left so little."

"Why didn't you impart more?"
"Why didn't you relish life more?"
"You had time."
 "Look, here they come!"
"Your families and friends have arrived."
"They took their time but here they are."
"Look, my children!"
"And over there are friends I haven't seen in … years…"
 "My parents, what are they doing here?"
"They passed long ago…"
 "Whose gravestone are they reading?"
"Oh no…oh God…"
"It's mine…"
"Mine…"

Change

Time brings change
We forcefully resist
And never win
Exhausted we acquiesce

Smiles masquerade grief
We cry in anguish
Allowing burdens to impede
We quietly reflect on, "what ifs"

Change once accepted
Is victory celebrated
Empowering ourselves
Replacing pity with potentiality

Cock Fight

Smoke as thick as a summer fog
Floated over my head
Swirls of it grabbed my suit
Clawing through its fabric
To lick my flesh
Like a thick tongued whore
I knew I'd smell like
An ashtray after leaving
This sweat and piss bucket of an arena
The hacking beanpole of a man
Who'd, led me here demanded his,
¡Cinco dolarés!
He snatched the bill
And pushed into the horde of gamblers
The arena was not large
Dried blood in splotches
Splattered on the small circular wall
Fighting cocks were proudly hoisted
Into the air for all to see
Magnificent feathers gleamed
In vibrant colors of dark blues, greens
Oranges and reds
Under the bright hot light
Then unceremoniously dropped
Into the center of the ring
Loud screams of encouragement
Whistling and laughter filled the air
One could hardly think or concentrate
The action was furious
Rapid, sharp barbs
Cut into rooster flesh spraying blood
Within seconds it seemed
A winner was raised
Into the air once more
Suddenly the crowd became

Alarmed and retreated to an exit
As policemen blew whistles
And beat their batons on the unprotected
A man pushed and shoved
Past me and yelled into my ear,
"Someone brought a dick to the cock fight!"
I laughed at his unintended pun
While joining the frantic mob at an exit

Conclusion

The answer for us is always the same
The fool takes his time because his thoughts are dim
While the intellectual's denials are cloaked in paradigms
My dear friends,
In the end humanity, reaches the same conclusion
Death after all, is no illusion

Cowboy

Calls himself a cowboy
Riding lonesome and loco
In a wild and crazy world
Of suits and ties
Riding stainless steel stairs
Staring at two-way glass
Concrete rodeo
Short of ponies and colts
No pistol belt or six-gun
Roustabout in jeans and boots
Bronco busting city gals
"Cow poking" he laughs
When lassoing full-figured gals
Instead of skinny glamour dolls
Makes fun of everyone
Ignoring his reflection
Western hat looking strange
Riding in a mini-van
Floorboard full of beer bottles
Modern city without cattle
Drunk and belligerent
Chewing on a plug
Spitting on carpet
Doesn't give a damn
Calls himself a cowboy
Though he's from Vietnam

Crumbs

Crumbs litter the table
Nourishment for a hungry soul
My anticipated feast awaits
Your departure

Discards in a box
A treasure trove
A pauper today
A king tonight

Scraps for the taking
Wardrobe for a languished brain
Stained seersucker suit, shirts and pants
Ties of mouthwatering colors

Dumpster delights
A wealth of opportunity
A bum tonight
A businessman tomorrow

Dark Cold 45

Smiling boldly
Weaving past
Piss pant drunkards
Droopy eyed druggies
Gypsies and pimps
Dressed all in black
Biting her lip
Eyes wide as saucers
Not expecting the worst
But prepared nonetheless
Finger on trigger
Of a dark cold 45
Lady's got courage
Girl's got some class
Not afraid to give birth to
A new hole upside your ass
Keep your hands
To yourselves men
Best watch your step
Don't give her, no shit man
She keeps smiling boldly
With a feeling of power
Skipping past gum smacking
Pregnant whores
Selling what's left
Of themselves
The dregs of the earth
Perverted old and young men
Eye her like pie
She' soft and gentle
With a dark cold 45

Death Smiled A Silly Grin

This flu's too much
For me to handle
Kicking my ass
With snot and headache
Feels like I've fought fifteen rounds
Breathing's short and rough
Treadmill tough
Marathon dry lungs
Hurt with each breath
Can't talk without
Blowing blood
Through wet nostrils
Throat hacks dryly
Knees aching
Back hobbled
Looking like death
In need of a rest
Looking skeletal
Dragging sickle
Towards another poor soul
Ready to kick and fight back
My reflection on the mirror
Says it's time for bed
I grab tissues, medicine
A cup of herbal tea
And blankets, lots of blankets
As my eyes close
I see a figure at the door
Nooo not now… I'm too tired…
But I can't break this date
Death smiled a silly grin
Then vomited
On my floor

Discarded Lives

Torn souls
Ripped from loving arms
Lost minds
Swollen with useless knowledge
Sore frames
Resting between thin sheets
Discarded lives should not disturb
Our pleasant thoughts

Dashed hopes
Slip past our future
Truths caught
In webs of lies
Hollow dreams
On restless nights
Discarded lives cannot distract us
From our projected goals

Annihilated people
Of a lesser world
Weather dried tears
On decaying corpses
Blood poured forth
From shrinking hearts
Discarded lives do not touch
The hearts in the best of us

Do You Believe?

Fate
Destiny
Fortune
Do you believe?

We dream and work for fortune and fame.
When suddenly faced with these ideals,
We thank our lucky stars.

Curses
Bad luck
Doom
Do you believe?

Failing our goals believing ourselves ruined,
We blame misfortune.
Distraught, we shake a fist heavenward at our accursed luck.

Do you believe?

Dozing Into Nightmare

Sleeping like a dead man
Fevered nightmares burning
Through my aching head
Fingers curled into fists
Fighting like a boxer
With the devils of Hell
I wake up sweating
And shaking
And hear my girlfriend
Snoring like a bear
Caught in a trap
She's dozed off in a chair
Warmed by a blanket
Of her jet black hair
Knees and face pressed together
Slobbering like a mad dog
Should wake her
But she'll get rabid
Darkness comes back
I'm dozing into nightmare
Afraid of the devils
I jump out of bed
Don't want to go back
To hell
May not come back
Next time

Dreams And Sanity

Our minds fear insanity
Understanding abnormal
Is a power we've long desired
But little comprehend
Average thoughts are safer
Nothing beyond that
Or panic grips
Shaking our being
Am I sane?
What is sanity?
Dreams predict
What may come
Should I wait?
Take action?
Taken as truth
Prediction becomes real
Fears become realities
Insanity turns sane
Sanity is normal
Dreams told me so
They've shown me the way
No one else knows
As I know
The truth
And you don't
And never will
Because you don't dream
You told me so
In a nightmare
Of reality so real
I could taste the air
And it was you
It was you
Who told me to stop dreaming
And make things happen

So why don't you dream?
Are you sane?
I know I am
I predicted you
And here you are
Making things happen

Drop Box

Eyeglasses
Hearing Aids
Cellular phones
Walking canes
An aluminum one with
Plastic handle used once
An older wooden cane
Sits next to the newer model
Worn, faded black
Almost green as the yellow pine
Peeks through from use
A life in need of assistance
Gone from this earth now,
And all that remains
Is a reminder in a drop-box
At your local grocery store

Empty Bottles

My son's eyes were so sad and innocent
Genaro, stood next to my bed and pleaded
"Daddy, don't drink, I don't like it."
Hung-over and filled with remorse, I could only nod

My own father had been alcoholic all of his adult life
Growing up we never spoke about it
And if I had, he would've been incapable
Childhood for my sisters and I had been quite fearful

Empty bottles lay about
Devoid of their alcoholic spirits
And now, as I surveyed the remains of the party
I suddenly felt devoid of spirit

My son's plea awoke within me
All of the painful memories I thought I'd outgrown
The pain and fear were as vivid today as they were back then
My son of five, helped me to stop drinking, I cannot thank him enough

Enough

Mothers...
Have you not heard enough?
Why do you wait?
We, your sons and daughters are crying!

Sisters...Brothers...
Have you not had enough?
When will you help end the carnage?
Are there no tears in your eyes?
We, your sisters and brothers are bleeding!

Spouses...Lovers...
Have you not seen enough?
Where is your love, your compassion?
Is your soul devoid of peace?
We, your lovers and spouses are dying!

Yes, the towers fell they are gone
Our fears have somehow dissipated.
Still American lives bleed
In the mountains and deserts of foreign lands
And here, you laugh and entertain yourselves
Like all is normally and morally fine

Eons

Walking for eons over hot grainy sands
Caught falling stars with my bare hands
Eyes filled with beauty and so much more
World full of mysteries all mine to explore
Dreamed liquid amber from drinking wild
Cracked jokes that cracked many a smile
Your tawny body completely sun baked
Heart stuck in my throat dry and blood-caked
Stared as you danced naked and bold
Hands of a stranger hot yet cold
Horses stampede in my mind's eye
Gliding through thunderous dark purple sky
With machete in hand, tore and hacked
At barriers built to press us back
Verdant jungles of hot humid danger
Confusion, frustration, madness and anger
Smiling grandly while saving your soul
Coating my body with blood drawn from a bowl
Hating all art, their painters and wits
Objects I'd rather paint with my fists
Begging and yelling at the top of my lungs
Blindly grabbing at oil coated rungs
Flailing at demons that rip at my chest
Praying for angels and much needed rest
Broiling sun slowly burning me dry
Children laugh while watching me cry
Heart squeezed anger primed to explode
Bearing a painful volatile load
Soft soothing song put me at ease
Fill my soul with wonderful peace
Martyrs and saints sharp crosses drawn
Lunatics chasing me past perfect dawn
Black-spotted Panther poised to attack
Vengeful Indios aim for my back
Frantic and feverish, saddle heavy with gold

Nowhere nearer am I to my goal
Running for eons over hot grainy sands
Caught falling stars with my bare hands

Even The Sun Cried

With a voice as soft as his heart
His strong hand guided us through our fears
His beautiful smile a bright beacon
Led us to safe harbor
Giving us no choice but to follow

His most powerful tools were;
Understanding, forgiveness and patience
Virtues which brought us to the brink of love
He taught like no other giving of himself
His students were unsurpassed, the elite

Our hearts cried out in grief the day he fell
For he was more than a teacher, he was our friend
And as the angels triumphantly embraced him
The earth and moon trembled with such joy
That even the sun cried

(From the play, "Even The Sun Cried")
Written and Produced by Manuel Nava Leal

Everyday People

Fred and I
Drink warm beer
Watching the sun set
As crowds gather
Across the street
Concrete barb-wired walls
Loom over
Everyday people
The pro, the con
In their jeans
Or Sunday best
A few hastily write
On bright poster board
Tacking their signs to wooden sticks
The con smile and nod to one another
Casually glancing our way
With disapproving frowns
Trying to draw us down
We simply smile
Tipping our bottles to them
Street lights
Push darkness away
Candles are lit
Silence ensues
Awaiting the pronouncement
A few shed tears
Some laugh and taunt
This isn't new
It happens often
Enough to be routine
Here in Texas
Fred and I
Drink warm beer
Watching the parade
Of everyday people

Feuding and holding
Their candlelight vigil
For the condemned

Fairy Dust

Delicate fairy
Sprinkle my child
With your fairy dust
Filling her fancy
With cheer

Dainty fairy
Blow her a kiss
With your fairy love
Granting her dreams
Without fear

Fall Leaves

Leaves fall all about
Dancing like miniature ballerinas through the autumn air
Delightfully pirouetting and flying
Anxiously vying for the perfect stage on which to land

The first to descend are sadly unable to display their turned coats
While the last, proudly exhibit the full spectrum of fall colors
They bow, content and at peace
Their final ballet, well received

First Born

On a dark still night
A first breath was heard
Your tenderness
Was felt

Souls shook with joy
At the sight of you
Tears cascaded from
Loving eyes

Sleep weary babe
Rest your tiny frame
The world anticipates
Your touch

Fisticuffs

Fisticuffs,
"Da Gentlemen's Sport,"
Was lessen dat
On dat olden day
We was bot bleedin
Like bust virgins
Me eyes cut open
By da nails in is gloves
Me mouf swollen
An cussing a storm
Wile he laught at me
Is feet was flat though
An heavy as clay
An drug roun da ring
Like a ton o'bricks
Still, is gloves foun
Mor o' me to poun an rip
T'was thru a hail o'blood
Swet an thunda
Dat I saws me way to im
T'was clear as da air
His left eye twinkled
Wit a tear
An I saws me chance
At last
I knowed right den
Jus how ta fist'm
Coupl'a rib shots
Some jabs
An more ribs
An a coupl'a a lef hooks too
A right to da mouf
An he fell like Goliat
Face first on da mat
Bounc a coupla times

Den no more
Da ref thrust me arm
In da air
An declare me da champ!
Wot joy!
Wot a relief

Fool

I never took myself
So seriously
Never understood
What it meant to be
A man
Don't take me wrong
It's just that
Sometimes I just
Got out of hand
I'm not a kid
Just been a fool

I laughed and played
Made fun of many
I didn't understand
What it was
To be a friend
It was wrong of me
To have been silly
To have been so callous
Simply put,
I was jealous
You see,
I've been a simpleton

It's taken me years
To comprehend
That my life too,
Has, had meaning
I've lost time and learned
That life is fleeting
I am no longer
That simple fool

Funny Things

All over my body, funny things are happening
My ears are sprouting hair as long as antennae
My nose is too!
What the heck did I do to deserve this?

All around me funny things are being said
Pardon me, what was that?
Would I like some cat hair?
Ohhhhh, caviar!
What the hell are my eardrums beating?

Funny things appear before my eyes
Like the beautiful young lady who winked flirtatiously at me
When I saw her up close and in the daylight, she was as old as
Granny!

Damn, I remember making fun of the elderly
What the heck did I do that for?

Gina's Dream

In her dream, Gina awakens
To find me standing on the threshold
Of her bedroom door

I'm smiling broadly
With outstretched arms and say, "It's time."
She, smiling just as much, rises to hug me

She says she no longer wants
To live with her mother and live-in boyfriend
He tears are huge as she embraces me tightly

In reality, as she speaks those words, I cry
My heart aches so much so that I cannot speak
How can I tell her it's not possible?

Her mother has to consider what is best for Gina,
She'd never give her consent
There is far too much to lose

If I could only make my daughter's dream a reality
I know her smile would return and not be as sad
And she'd no longer cry as when I return her presently

One day, Gina's dream will come true

For my daughter, Gina Ann

God's Covenants

You honored us with life,
Creating us from clay
Love's joys
Were thankfully experienced
Your guarantee of suffering,
Sorrowfully humbling
The compact of peace,
Gratefully accepted
Your promised return,
Anxiously awaited

Gulf Coast Treasures

Crowds are to be tolerated by others
I'd rather go for long walks
Along lonely stretches of the Gulf Coast
I'm blessed to know of such places
Where I can indulge in peaceful contemplation
And those like a miser I'll cling to, tightly
Those sanctuaries of solitude are so few today
That they are as precious as gemstones
Forgive my reticence in divulging
My Gulf Coast treasures

Half After He's Done

Cars and trucks whiz past
As the sun rises in the east
Light rays open your eyes
To find me on the truck bed
Swinging my legs like a child
As night disappears before me
Traffic continues rushing past
No one seems to care
That we're stranded
No one dares look our way
We don't exist
They are not our salvation
Is it the Texas plates?
The gun rack, that holds no guns?
Is it me, you or is it both of us?
We must look menacing
Stranded here in our Sunday best
The flares burnt out long ago
Way before the sun smiled
At our predicament
One lone cop car
Without its siren wail or flashing lights
Blew past, obliviously
I shook my head
Jumped off the truck bed
And put out the cigarette under my toe
Drank the last few drops of soda
Squeezing the weak can in disgust
"When did people stop caring?"
"Where the hell are they rushing off too?"
You smiled and shook your fist in the air
In solidarity of my rhetorical questions
As I gathered our things
Preparing to leave our truck
In this lonely spot

Full of passing motorists
An old lady pulls up
"Trouble?" she asks
Through a partially open window
"Just a little," you answer with a shy smile
"Boyfriend's not much of a Chanic, is he?"
"No ma'am he's not," smiling broadly now
Embarrassed, I look down towards my boots
Thumbs tightly clenching my belt loops
"I'll send my boy!" she yells raising the window
"We'll wait!" I call to her
"How long?" you manage before she drives away
She suddenly brakes forcing the car to rock forward
"Half after he's done!" and speeds off
Tearing into the traffic
Like a shark on the prowl
"Half after he's done?"
We both say simultaneously
We stare at each other quizzically
And burst into laughter
We lay back down on the truck bed
Staring at vast flocks of birds
Looking like hundreds of tiny freckles
Dotting the huge orange sun
Anxiously waiting for,
"Half after he's done."

Hatred of Me

I'm thinking of stepping out
Before I pull my hair and shout
Simply running away
The struggle for companionship
Has given our relationship
A reason for dismay
I feel the hatred of an ex
Swaying over my head
Like a terrible hex
Tell me the truth don't lie
You know you want
To stab me in the eye
Were we married in the past?
Did I anger you that fast?
Your eyes are staring me a hole
Like murder is your goal
I feel the hatred of an ex
My mind is hurting
My soul is vexed

Hiding In Innocence

Cherubic smile
Caresses dimpled cheeks
Naiveté personified
Concealing sinful thought
Or mischievous act

Angelic aura
Irradiates virtuous visage
Saintliness exemplified
Obscuring vanity
Hiding in innocence

Highway Breakdown

The road goes on forever
With the stars blazing all around
I don't want this ride to end, never
Full moon trails me to town
Blue moon keeping me down

Wheels tear up the black tar
Heat raising the hog's bar
No way to make town
Nothing living all around
Damned highway breakdown
Damned highway breakdown

Sun burns right through me
As my hands twist and turn tools
Pain burns my back and knees
Damned heat's for lizards and mules
The desert is for dead men and fools

Wheels tear up the black tar
Heat raising the hog bar
No way to make town
Nothing living all around
Damned highway breakdown
Damned highway breakdown

If I don't make it into town
It was the sun that took the kill
Tell them to have another round
Cause there's never been a better thrill
Than the dead man's ride in the desert chill

Damned highway breakdown
Damned highway breakdown

House Without Shadows

White walls and doors
Ceilings and floors
Bright lights
Shine on every corner
"House without shadows"
Is how it is known
The few who've gone in
Swear there's
Not a dark spot anywhere
Not the halls
Cupboards or shelves
Closets or bathroom stalls
White paint and light
Bathe everything
Night never kisses a window
Dark never had a chance
Moon better be full
The sun better
Not take a break
If a shadow appears
It will be blasted
With handheld light
The owner's eccentric
They say
But that's not the cause
Seems she was
Raised in a basement
From birth to eight
In the house without shadows
Light is her pleasure
If you ask me,
She's fighting off fright

In A Mall

In a mall teeming with consumers
I sit alone and write
South American accents
Fill the air to my left
A loud and sudden hand clap startles....
An explosion of nervous laughter soon follows
An anxious mother furrows her brow
As her teenage daughter eyes a tiny dress
Bored and lonesome booth-keepers
Whisper secrets into cell phones
While smiling awkwardly at passersby
Dark happy indigenous faces mingle
Amid brightly colored clothes
Surprising smiles from wide-eyed toddlers
Who without warning, shriek piercingly
It's three o'clock on a Sunday afternoon
Feeling lost and lonely
In a mall teeming with consumers

In The Corner Of Our Darkness

There is a space in each of us
A momentary quietness
A place without echoes
Where we retreat
In silent contemplation
To cleanse our tongue
Wash our soul
Open our mind's eye
Revel in warm blood
The thump thumping
Of our heart
The only sound
We cower in the corner
Of our darkness
Where there are no reflections
To prejudice our eyes
Truth is finally revealed
And the hot air that surrounds us
Smells heavy with dread
Giving off proof
Of our deep seated fear
Though we suppress mightily
We know that
In that corner of our darkness
We hide in fear of the light
The reason
For our existence

Inspirational

Finding inspiration is easy
An odd couple makes me wonder
Just as much as the perfect one
A frown, a smile, a tear, a laugh
Sounds, colors, silence
A betrayal cleansed my heart and soul
Like nothing had before
Words of hatred and such pain
Split my lips and mind in two
Inspiration none the less
Love found me spouting
Words I'd not imagined
Never written in heartfelt moments
Loneliness, my God
Loneliness inspires more
Than just about anything
Life, above all
Is truly inspirational

Justice, Hope, Reality

Justice is myth
Dispensed
Not only by angels
But demons of jest

Worshiping hope
As though
By will alone
Wrongs might be righted

Multi-dimensional reality
Confusing our minds and tongues
By word and belief
As truths rip our hearts asunder

Justice, Hope and Reality
A nightmare and a dream
Unleashed on our being
By specters of halo and wing

Life Stones

If I am not the cornerstone of my own foundation
What good am I to you?

If not the keystone of your life
What am I to you then?

Will my soul be crushed like meal
By the doubts of love's millstone?

Heave my soul over the precipice
Pray I become a rolling stone

Elevate me to what I have dreamt
And I will be far more than a steppingstone

I am not, yet mere words carved on a tombstone
I am that I am and dare not cast the first stone

Madness…All is Madness!

Madness courses through me
Thoughts sliced thin
As if by menacing razor
No blood
No orientation
All is freewheeling mayhem
Standing is impossible
Sitting a crime
Kneeling forbidden
Seeing without comprehension
Sounds rave and bounce randomly
Fever sears my flesh
Like an inferno
Body and soul stink of brimstone
Madness…all is madness!
Light forever extinguished
I quiver and shake uncontrollably
Erotic visions burn
Memories deeply ingrained
Erasing them impossible
Blood extinguishes desire
Lust fades like dusk
A bed of thorns
Awaits my sleep
Hellfire my sunrise
Happiness a hollow trick
Darkness…all is darkness!
Love never embraced
Simply teased
Claws wrench my bones
Teeth rip my skin
Pain is all too familiar
The only thing I understand
My love, my solace
Failure…all is failure

Memories

Days become lost
Like seconds in an hour
Times are seen as though
Through thinnest veil
Certain memories
A mere few
Retain their clarity
Only those that
Through our own care
And desire are recalled
To sooth and caress our hearts
Bringing us back
To fond moments
With precious visions
And feelings so strong as to
Reduce us to weeping
Or seduce us with laughter
Memories are dreamscapes
Emblazoned in our
Hearts and minds
With the power
To remind us
Of who we once were
And whom we once knew

More Time

Time is gliding by so effortlessly
Almost imperceptibly
Our passage is like
The last ember slowly cooling, fading
Yet we ride it wildly, blindly almost
Suddenly looking back wondering
How? How could this be?
I was merely a child days ago
Falling in love only yesterday
Yet tomorrow seems so close at hand
What will it bring?
A scowl to ward off others and
Cold recollections of loneliness?
Or perhaps a contented smile
And a heart full of loving memories?
We go into our time
Wearing that which we choose
Will we find ourselves alone?
Or with glad company in that sweet tomorrow?
Alone we depart never the less
And then shall find that we
Have ridden time at such a pace
As to make us contemplate
How? How could this be nearly over?
I've just now opened my eyes, my mind!
Why did I, sit passively
Staring at the hourglass
As time sifted away so smoothly?
Why did I, fail to save
A few grains of sand for living?
How could I, have allowed myself
To be lead by others
Instead of trusting my inner voice?
I will boldly run
The remainder of my course

To its allotted destination
And pray to be allowed more time
No matter that I finish last or first
As either way
I'll end up winning

Morocco

Sand grates every fold of my body
The tinniest wrinkles can be felt
Sweat helps create rivulets of mud
I'm standing on a dune, one of many

The setting sun paints a red tableau
Engulfing all, including the darkest shadow
Sounds and scents gently waft towards me
An undulating prayer call arises from the city

My dreams of coming here are realized
Longing for this place of ancient history
Is now relieved and I laugh in disbelief
Enjoying every fragment of this experience

Like a child building its first sandcastle
My soul is filled with elation and wonder
Neither sand nor heat dare disturb my happiness
Morocco…
The name is so inviting

My Seven Paths

First Path:
Innocence, Fear, Dependence

Second:
Curiosity, Question, Defiance

Third Path:
Independence, Experiment, Offense

Fourth:
Strife, Neglect, Abandon

Fifth Path:
Possession, Release, Reflect

Sixth:
Curiosity, Question, Defiance

Seventh Path:
Innocence, Fear Dependence

My Son

Yes, he isn't perfect
We knew that
Before the adoption
You threw him out
Not once but twice
Like you would trash
My son
Your reject

He is much more
Than you will ever know
His pain is immeasurable
But I will love him
And not discard him
No matter the sacrifice
My son
Your yesterday's news

I will see him
At his best
He will be a good man
A great father
He will love and be loved
He will survive
My son
Your loss

Now

Hard to tell now
But I was once
Mean
Crazy mean
Vicious
Looking for trouble
Stab you without cause
Just mean

Hard to tell now
But there once was a time
When I was unhappy
Stubborn
Bitter
Clinically depressed
Suicidal

Not hard to tell
That now I'm
Caring
Kind
Giving
Thoughtful
Seriously kind of sane

One…

One frown can extinguish a warm smile.

One callous remark brings hurt to a vibrant soul.

One canceled date can cause great despair.

One pointed finger can stab to the bone.

One cold shoulder can freeze a yearning heart.

One vulgar word can dash a dream.

One vain laugh can shut an open mind.

One idea repressed can dam inspiration.

One rejection can bring on a torrent of tears.

One love can cure all.

One Day

There will come a day
When everyone
Will walk on water

That day arrives
And we will understand
The meaning of life

One day
There will be a revolution
A revelation of the soul

The day will come
When love
Will conquer hate

One day...
The day...
We succumb to death

Onward Upward

We strive
To step
Lock step
Look up
Rise up
Climb up
Shimmy up
Push up
Pull up
Don't be
Washed up
Onward
Upward
Higher
And higher
Never give up
Never look down
Never screw up
Never lose ground
Hurry up
Scurry up
Face up
Chin up
Heads up
Buck up
Don't be
A fuck up
Onward
Upward
Higher
And higher
We strive

Papers

ICE asked for my passport
The border crossing
Less than a hundred feet away
Told them I hadn't gotten one yet
No smile, no welcome back
After a few questions
They tossed me my driver's license
They grudgingly let me through
"Must have checked on warrants,"
I said to no one
Smiling, I found myself
Back in the USA
I felt uneasy though
Watching a boy of about six
Crying at his grandmother's crossing
Going back to Mexico
Heading back home
"Buela," he cried,
"Tell Abuelito,"
"I can't see him anymore!"
"Tell him I'm just like Daddy now,"
"I don't have papers!"
He cried louder
As his mother picked him up
Holding him high
For just one wave to Grandma
And a wipe of his eyes and nose
"Tell him I don't have papers."
The sound of that ironic plea
Brought shame and anger
What has our country become?
When *American* kids
Can't see their relatives
Without a passport?
Without papers

What have we become
What have we become

Pearl Button

Rainbow of glimmering color
Where light touches your surface
Found entwined in the roots of a fallen tree
Red clay embedded in slight imperfections
Pearl button in otherwise excellent shape
Delicate survivor of years long gone
Buried in the soil of an antebellum plantation
What was your purpose?
Who did you belong to?
What fashionable material did you hold fast?
Who carved you from shell?
How did you end up beneath that tree?
Will you reveal secrets of the past?
Your discovery intrigues

Pennies In The Grass

I found a handful
Of pennies in the grass
Near a children's slide
New shiny copper
Glistened
Through green blades
On this sunny
Summer day
A tiny treasure
Waving at me
From a distance
Inviting their discovery
Lincoln smiled
Over and over
As though
Happy to be found

Promise

Today brought with it
A storm of renewal
Torrential thoughts poured
Through my mind
And past my lips
Ideas of such huge potential
That my body quivered
With enthusiasm
Sharing these thoughts
With you
Renews my spirit
Making me believe
Myself capable of anything
That the future
Does indeed
Hold promise

Pumice Stone

Squeeze my heart dry
With delicate hands
Use it as you would
Pumice stone
Wipe your soul pure
Of pretension and fear
Soak in the blood
Of my essence
Except its sensual caress
Quench your desires
In my enduring love
Of your bounty
And with delicate hands
Hold fast the pulse
Of my beating heart
Use it as you would
Pumice stone

Push and Pull

A breeze visits
My back
Interrupting
My thoughts
My daydream
As I sat
Studying the swish
And sway
Of branches
Pushed and pulled
By the wind
Treetops wiping
The sky clear
Of dust
And cloud
Jacket open
Turning to face
The interloper
Inviting the cool embrace
I smiled in earnest
As the clear blue palette
Is suddenly splattered
With multi colored leaves
Flying as legion towards
What their, next life?
To be trampled upon
Decaying beneath those
That, ignore their beauty?
Laying on the warm ground
Resting my eyes I listen
As death and life
Dance to the
push and pull.
Of a breeze

Rain Dance

Rain mercilessly
Pelts them
As they slip slide and skip
Over curbs and
Floating obstacles
Thunder roars approval
Of the rain dance
Umbrellas dot the streets
Like multi-colored leaves
Drifting downstream
Water rooster-tails over
A sidewalk ballerina
Who gracefully pirouettes off
Thoughtless drivers
Spray the already
Rain-soaked crowd
Who shake their fists
And curse aloud
At darkened skies
While children
Cheerfully close their eyes
Tilt their heads
And open-jawed
Lick raindrops
From silver edged
Swollen clouds

Rain Spirit

Spirit of rain
Pelt my soul
With nourishing
Raindrops
Engulf me wholly
For I
Am dry
Fill me
With your
Pure water
For I
Am parched
I am
Desert
Beat my ground
Like a drum
Oh Rain Spirit
Sprinkle your
Wonder drops
Make my cactus bloom
Wet the dust
Fill all cracks
To overflowing
With your
Pure and holy water
Hear me
Rain Spirit
Heal me
Rain Spirit
Bring your thunder
To the deafness
Wake the dead
Inundate
My parched soul
Oblige my plea
Oh Rain Spirit

Read It Again

Do you recall past friends?
Tell who they were!

Were you there when it happened?
Tell us again?

Where in the world did you go?
Take us there too!

Have you seen the past, present and future?
We want to know!

Did you memorize a favorite passage?
Recite it once more!

Remember our favorite story?
Read it again! Read it again!

Remember Benny

"El Gordito,"
Ran for his life
Jiggling bare fat belly
Spraying hot sweat at every turn
Head full of black spiked hair
Standing out like thick nopal needles,
Glistening with morning dew
His face turned toward us
Frightened eyes full of tears
His mouth wide open
Foaming at the edges
Screamed like a "niña,"
As Chito grabbed his stubby neck
And Freddie tackled him
At the knees, they fell
"Tres chamacos," rolling on hot asphalt
The powerful revving motor
Stopped me cold
Chito and Freddie fell away in time
The memory of
Steel against soft flesh
Brings tears to my eyes
Years later as I remember Benny
"El Gordito"
Memories of a friend
Who'll never be forgotten
"Chase" became a deadly game
Frozen in a tragic instant

I still pray for Benny.

Reminisce

Remember tears
They renew your strength

Recall pain
It built immunity

Reflect on disappointments
To improve relationships

Reminisce on the good
Reaffirming your life

Riding

I experience the sensation of absolute freedom
Pedaling my bike rapidly on the old highway
The broiling sun has melted the top layer of tar
Making it soft and sticky
So that it hisses as I roll along
I smile listening to that sound
No longer having to walk on it barefoot
A hot breeze hugs my back
Between open shirt and bare skin

Trampled frogs line the road near the arroyo
Zigzagging trying to avoid them
I suddenly swerve to avoid a dead skunk
The stench fills my lungs,
So I pedal faster to clear them
A truck loaded with melon suddenly swerves around me
The angry driver screams and waves a solitary finger
I wave back but with both hands
As the brake lights come on
I quickly cut through an empty lot

The cantina already has clients,
The jukebox blasts out Norteñas while they drink
There are empties to crate and messes to clean
The broom is almost worn to the stick,
But Berta "La Tacaña," won't buy a replacement
"Mañana," she grumbles
A shiny new car parks next to the old trucks and cars
A beer salesman winks at me as he strolls up to Berta
She smiles and pretends to be grateful as he hands her
Posters and calendars of bikini-clad beauties

I experience the satisfaction of a job well done
As I pedal through the cantinas' parking lot
The broiling sun has heated the loose gravel
Making it dry and brittle
So that it crackles as I roll along
I smile listening to that sound
No longer having to walk on it barefoot
A hot breeze hugs my back
Between open shirt and bare skin

Run

Run from the scorching sun
Do not pause or you will burn
And the ash that once was you
Will blow away with a summer's breeze

Run from the blazing sun
Don't dare stop to catch your breath
Or it will snatch and melt your soul
As though you never were

Run from the frying sun
Don't dare glance into it's face
There is no turning back
You only existed because of it

Run from the sun…Run from the sun
Run from the sun…Run from the sun…
Run from the sun…run…run…run…run…

Shadow

Skipping way in front of me
Is my shadow
It can't help itself
As though needing to know
What lies before me
When the brilliant sun shines
It runs so far ahead
At times edging around corners
Wanting to tear free of me
Feeling perhaps like an interloper
But we arrive together
As Siamese twins
Not separate yet equal
On cold cloudy days
My shadow pulls itself in close
So as to be warm and invisible
On moonlit nights
Shadow runs ahead once more
Seeking companionship elsewhere
And nights when there is no moon
My shadow hides within
Like a tiny child afraid of the dark
Only peering out at candlelight
Those times I share with a friend
Shadow brings along a partner
Like double dating, afraid to be alone
But when I've had enough
I close the door, turn off the light
That I may have some privacy

Shadow Messages

Light creeps slowly towards darkness
Seeking shadows to destroy
Darkness is unholy
And should be exposed
Its nature revealed
Shadows lurk around us
Following our very steps
Miming our every move
Dark shadows remain cool
Unobtrusive
Their presence, obscure
Unclear, mysterious
When light destroys shadows?
Who shall mourn dark's passing?
Will tears be shed?
Shadow messages will cease
Black will move no more
Damn the brightness!
Curse the light!
It is crude, course
Inquisitive
It burns through
What we'd rather hide
Restrain the light!
Refuse passage to the place
Where shadows dance naked
Happily relishing life
Caressing our secrets
Shielding us from insult
Damned light is harsh, intrusive
Unforgiving
Extreme to our imperfections
Why fear the dark?
It is only the antithesis of light
Shadows should be sheltered

Tendered, kissed
We must revel in beautiful darkness
Refusing the light which bares
Our faults and failures
Our realities

Shangri-La

Wisteria winds through a snow white trellis
Arched above a wicker bench and chairs
A swath of lush green interlaced with white and lavender blossoms
Cascading like twin waterfalls on opposite sides

A Shangri-La of scent and colorful attractions
Tempting the most delicate of butterflies
That flit and flutter daintily
In their idyllic ballet of delight

Hummingbirds and bumblebees impossibly balanced
Courteously allow one another a taste of the sweetest juices
While noisy and lumbering humans arrive
To relax with glasses full of their kind of nectar

Shattered and Scattered

Thoughts roll like tumbleweeds
Rambling past
Mesquite and cactus
Clawing at them as they near
Bouncing into the air
Round as the sun
Wishing to take flight
To escape to a verdant land
A world to which they don't belong
Looking and feeling out of place
Eventually yearning for home
Praying to return
Hoping for a breeze
A wind gust to send them back
No ruby slippers
No heels to click
Homesick and forlorn
Boundless introspection
Thoughts and more thoughts
Too much stimuli
Thinking too much
Thinking too little
Thinking I think
Contemplation on being
Such are the rambling musings
Of a philosopher without theology
No God leading the pack
A life with form and little control
No scientific evidence explains
The many mistakes
Too little success
How do you weigh science?
How much does it weigh?
Imagine no gravity
No gravy on the train

Where was I?
Where was I going?
Oh yeah
Thoughts fly
I fly
The fly thought
Flies think I think
Do they care?
I don't think I care
I think too much
I'll let them fly
My thoughts, I mean
I can be mean
I am meaningfully meaningless
Without meaning to be
I am mean, I mean to tell you
I mean it
Know what I mean?
Do you mind?
Should we be so mindful?
I mind
What is the philosopher's dilemma?
Existence
Or philosophers wouldn't exist
I crave mental stimulus
Ruminations on life
Self analysis
What controls us?
What, am I?
Who am I?
Why am I?
I worry,
Therefore I am a wart
Where do I fit in?
Does this fit?
Is there enough space?
What is my place?

Do we belong on this planet?
My world is a globe
As round as a tumbleweed
Is life like tumbleweed?
Or are my thoughts?
I forget
Why?
Why not?
It's synonymous
Aren't we rolling to the next thing?
The next best thing
End over end
Over and over again
In the dry deserts of the mind
Where dry winds blow
And dirt devils whirl
And once in a while
It rains
My head hurts
I need a break
My fragile thoughts lie
On the desert landscape
Shattered and scattered

Slumber

Our child
Slumbers amid
A stuffed menagerie of
Lions and tigers
And bare feet

Songs of the Tree and Bush

Majestic Saguaro, reluctantly surrender to the infernal desert heat
While the Palm and Palmetto clap a steady rhythmic beat

Swashbuckling Cedar and Redwood fenced one another
As the Pine and Hay jokingly needled each other

The Willow sadly weeps at the loss of "her partner, her tree,"
The carefree Cypress sat back in the swamps exposing their knees

Thorn bush and Cacti taunted everyone proving themselves, "Pricks,"
Sorghum stood next to Sweet-gum blowing bubbles with chewing-
gum sticks

Up north, the Conifers all frozen solid, "Those poor saps!"
Whilst, equatorial Jungles and Rainforests are wiped off the maps

Mahogany and Ebony cynically smile through their hardened hearts
Gossiping over Holly and Mistletoes' caressing and kissing, never
apart

Down in the hot, humid South, suffer the sweet Sugarcane
For the Maple trees further up north their bleeding partners in pain.

Hazelnut, Walnut, Chicory and Pecan, incessantly drive themselves
nuts
as Banana who clung to the tree like a monkey, giggled and watched

Good hardy Mesquite, Hickory and Oak smoked deeply, inhaling
down to the root
Never-minding the sensitive Pear, Apple and Peach who were bear-
ing fruit

A tiny Bonsai, inscrutably gazed up in wonder at the height of an un-
fettered tree
And thought to itself, *"I wish that could be me."*

Southeast Texas Fall

Hardly ever snows
In this part of Texas
But, we can tell it's cold up north of us
Cause the geese are honking overhead

The air gets cold here
Enough to see your breath float away
Frost appears on the grass, looks nice
Doesn't last long though, ground's still too warm

Leaves do normally turn about now,
Seems only the tallow are the most colorful
The trees eventually shed
Helping us see further

Vehicles sound nearer then before
They aren't any closer, the air only thinned
That same cool air brings morning fog
Making the earth appear to have risen to the clouds

Sun is moving further south now, making life cooler
Days are shorter causing us to dress warmer
Maybe this year it'll snow
Sure would be special

Staples on the Floor

Staples on the floor, is an analogy. Management personnel have a tendency to demean lower level employees with "little mistakes."

Example:

A clerical employee is hard at work inputting statistics onto a spreadsheet from reams of documents stacked on the desk before him. As he removes staples, he tosses one towards the trash bin but misses. Rather than picking it up right then, and knowing there will probably be more following, he returns to his work at hand. A supervisor observes what has happened and casually walks over and admonishes the clerk for tossing staples on the floor causing a safety concern. The clerk concentrating on avoiding clerical errors is now agitated and worried about an inconsequential distraction. He acknowledges the admonition but cannot focus on his previous task. The supervisor can now expect to see clerical errors that otherwise may not have occurred.

On finding errors in the reports submitted by the once admonished employee, the supervisor calls him to his office to now mete out amore severe tongue lashing, thus making the employee more nervous and agitated than before.
All due to "staples on the floor."

Synapses

Red, white and
Black curtains
Open to illusions
Behind shut eyes
Speckled with bursts
Of white, blues,
Purples and gold
Synapses
Separating our
Dreams from
The nightmares
Devouring our slumber
Throughout the night
Or the dreams
In our day
Imaginations are
Currents of synapse
Rivers of shock
Splitting delusions
Spitting illusions
Real is unreal
Unreal a reality
Uncertainty rules
Sleep is full of
Electrical bursts
Energized synapses
Visions with or without
Reason or rhyme
Dreams that come true
Are a memoriam
To time spent
Behind closed eyes

Tears

Tears streamed down her face like twin waterfalls
Light reflected off her nose
Her sad eyes red and swollen could scarcely keep from begging
She cried as I said my tearful goodbyes
Unable to contain her emotions she sobbed uncontrollably
I left her, knowing the she would find another
Someone else would fall in love with her soon enough
Cocker Spaniels have a way of finding homes sooner than most other breeds

The Box

I saw her holding the box behind her
That box is putting my mind to the test!
My patience can't wait for Christmas!
What could it contain?
Should I dare hope that it's for me?

She held it tightly in her arms
That box gives me no peace!
My curiosity won't cease!
I could sneak a peek later this evening
I'll have to wait with all my might!

She's put it down and walked away
That box is so annoying!
I can't put it off, I'm through toying!
It's time to solve this mystery
Oh no, it's empty!

The Final Song

Guilty soul render your alms
Heavier in heart than in one's arms
Quiet breathing begun in womb
Growing tenser as you sense the tomb
A life of ups and downs, rights and wrongs
Edging closer to the final song
In time these words too, shall fade
Along with the memories of our age
Will then the pages from which they sprang
Join the dreams, and hopes and prayers we sang?

Shallow breathing, silenced tongue
One step closer to the final rung
A lifetime of perpetual strife has brought
One life hostage to a dead-man's cot
Constant beating of a once strong heart
And vibrant thoughts will soon depart
What will happen with the final beat?
Will the soul live on, but feel incomplete?
Do we live on in people's dreams?
Will the spirit know then, what life means?

The Gentle Hailstorm

December was heavy with clouds
As I began my day on an early morning hunt
If I were further north instead of in Houston
I would have said that the clouds would bring snow this day

In the crook of my right arm rested my "partner,"
A metal detector I've hunted with for some time now
My left balanced a small shovel over my shoulder
My backpack nearly empty and light

The morning's dew had frozen
The grasses crunched and squeaked with every step
I was on terrain covered with tall pine trees
And wood fern that was caught off guard, lush and vibrant green

Scanning the purplish dark sky
I took notice of the quiet that engulfed my solitude
On this very ground during summer
The sounds of wildlife are loud and intense

My face felt the first raindrops
As I pulled the hood of my parka over my head
I came upon a fallen tree leaning against another
The rain soon became hail

The tapping sound of hail on frozen leaves was loud yet peaceful
I smiled lying back against that slanted tree
As the gentle hailstorm pelted my face
Wishing I could have shared that moment with a loved

The Scent Of Fear

Do I appear at all, frightened?
Do you smell dread?
Does the acrid scent
Like bitterly sharp adrenalin
Bite your tongue?
Do the hairs on the back of your neck
Rise like heat on a frosty morn?
Is it exciting?
Intoxicating?
Will the lioness in you
Leap at my jugular?
Will my warm blood fill your nostrils and soul?
Will it be enough to pacify your thirst?
Do my eyes reveal the coming loneliness
I know will be my eventuality?
Do you detect the scent of horror
Oozing through my pores?

The Sun Is Out

Emerald grass shimmers with moisture
Raindrops glitter as they cling to leaves
The sun is out
Fresh scent of rinsed soil lingers
Spring is back once again
Toads and frogs are content and silent
Allowing birds to whistle and sing
Gray clouds slowly open to a sky blue
Sunbeams play here and there on wet ground
Teasing and touching with warmth
The sun smiles as the earth laughs joyfully
Together bringing a rainbow reward

The Vertical Mirror

Revealing mirrors
draw us like magnets
Bouncing light flashing familiarity
rarely echoing the stranger

Features subtly change
yet, we continue to recognize
Time etching itself gently
waiting for the glass to crack

Flawed and perfected smiles
reflecting upon existence
Daily customs become rituals
ceremonies in walking the vertical mirror

They Survived

Dressed in poverty
Never begging or pleading
Not once asking for a handout
Toiling on empty stomach
Now and then
Never caused us
To rob or injure
Unfortunate, yet
We survived

The downtrodden live
Without bank account
Dignified but cashless
We pulled ourselves
Up by the bootstraps
Although strapless
Walked unless we bummed
A ride on a thumb, but
We survived

Scrutinized with pity
By the highbrowed
Created and perpetuated
By those privileged
The poor shall
Inherit the earth
Only at death
Our epitaph will read,
"They survived"

Thin Soup

Catching rain in tin cans
Shaving beans and garlic
Picking mushrooms to munch
Searching in trash bins
Thin soup today

No money, no roof, no matter
No place to go
Relaxing on cardboard
Relishing dinner
Thin soup, again

Time

About time
All the time
Behind the times
Chasing time
Closing time
Crying time
Daytime
Dead time
Double time
Full time
Fun time
Greenwich Time
Half time
Hang time
In time
Just in time
Jail time
Jolly ole time
Last time
Lonely time
Mass time
Missing time
Morning time
Moving time
Nap time
Nighttime
No time
Often times
Overtime
Part time
Pastime
Real time
Rest time
Run time
Siesta time

Sleepy time
Space Time Continuum
Time bomb
Timer
Timetable
Time of year
Time to go
Timepiece
War time
Wasted time
Wrinkle in Time

To You My Loving Daughter

How I love you, my delicate and gentle child
Softly breathing on my shoulder
Warmly nestled in your Daddy's arms

Sleep tenderly my daughter
And as you plumb the depths and breaths of dreams
I pray your future voyages are sweet and safe

May your winsome heart and guileless smile
Remain ever so innocent and dear, long after
I grudgingly release you unto this hardened world

Today's Mirror

Today's mirror hardly reflects who I am
Last night shocked me back to reality
I had begun to believe you
Your words revived a smile
I'd long ago lost in harsh memories
For years it hasn't been easy
Seeing my reflection
Often avoiding eye contact with myself
The few times I do, I cringe
Glancing at the ogre angrily staring back
How do you see differently?
I dared to look at my reflection
The other day I saw a smile, a tiny smile
I hadn't seen it in quite a while
But that was then
Today's mirror is blurred, refusing to reflect
Fearing the ogre's triumphant return
Your kind words were just an act
Confusing my reflection
But obviously, not for long

Toothless Grin

Tears of fright
Flow freely
A mixture of
Spit and blood
Cause trembling
A sudden realization
Brings on a toothless grin
A baby tooth
Thrust out
In a tiny palm

Top Of Your Game

Split open the curtain off the stage
Spit out words full of anger and rage
Screaming out verses like a Hindu Sage
Go on and holler your name!
You're at the top of your game!
You're at the top of your game!
And your hot sweat gleams
As the audience screams
Churned up like cream
It's risen to the top
Cause your words don't stop
So you sing the next verse
Feel like you're cursed
You shake your fist all about
You spit and you shout
Scream it out
To the world
Your about to explode
Like Chinese fireworks
That is lit to split
In a terrible roar
They still beg for more
Go on and holler your name!
You're at the top of your game!
You're at the top of your game!
Can't help yourself
Got to give it your all
So you sweat till you bleed
Giving more than they need
Spotlight dancing at your feet
They groove to the beat
They grovel at your feet
Got women in heat
You're at the top of your game
Go on and holler your name!

You're at the top of your game!
You're at the top of your game!

Trail Of Tears

Warmly caressing soft flesh,
Tears shed their moist skin as they flow
Leaving a tale of their wanderings
Exploding in watery fountains
Of laughter or pain
Wherever they fall
Absorbed by the earth
Or slowly evaporate
At their final destination
The trail of tears repeats
Leaving its mark as it cleaves
Through the bedrock of our lives
Like a constant and mighty river

Walls of Fire

We boldly walk
Through walls of fire
For love
Conviction
Redemption
Preservation
Purgation
Conversion
Perversion
Deception
In life
We blindly walk
Through walls of fire

What Can Be Said?

When thoughts of a friend come to mind,
Do you first imagine their face?
Or does a particular event or
Kindness come to mind?
Does the thought of that individual
Cause you to smile in reflection?

Special individuals come into our lives
Appropriately at times of most need.
Their presence is comforting, lifting us spiritually
Like proverbial angels coming to rescue or guide
Yes, they are angels brought to us by God.
Yet they blush and tears come easy at such words.

What can be said of such friends?
Words are inadequate and matter little to them.
What makes these friends smile and rejoice
Is your doing the same by serving others.
Honor and respect humanity
By humbling yourself.
Be a friend, like _____.

What Is New?

Everything is repeated
Ideas, thoughts, words
Today's humanity reveals nothing
That hasn't been proposed before
What is new?
Our past is our future
Our future our past
Computers?
They are a mode of conveyance
Words, brought to many
Faster, shinier, more colorful
But words and ideas just the same
What is new?
A child, but for how long?
At what point is a babe no longer new?
At first cry?
A series of firsts follows you till death
But are they new?
To you only.
All "firsts," have been experienced before
Humanity lives and dies repeatedly
 "Haven't you said, I've heard that before?"
"Doesn't dé-jà vu, sound familiar?"
Our dreams are an extension of our past
Images conveyed in blood, fluid and synapse
Experiences brought to us by ancestry
Sensory perceptions felt since time immemorial
What is new?

When We Know

It's easy knowing
What we want
It isn't easy
Letting go of things
Which harm, us
When we know
What's, best for us
The man you need
Turns out needy
The woman of your dreams
Becomes your worst nightmare
A goal you sought
Disappointed
The fight you won
Lost you a good friend
Your best drawn plan
Drew unplanned consequences
Life's experiences unfold
Revealing that your desires
May not be
What's, best for you
Somehow
A path is laid before us
Which we somehow follow
Bringing joy
To those with open minds
And sorrow
To those that don't admit
It isn't easy letting good of things
Which, harm us
Even when we know
What's, best for us

Why?

Huge tears fall
From my swollen eyes
As welts bleed
Through my shirt
The belt buckle
Hurt
But the words
The words were worse

Does my mother
Really, love me?
Why then, does she
Call me stupid?
Why does, she
Beat me?
Am I really
Just like my dad?

I look more
Like *her*
And, I'm a kid!
I don't drink,
I don't cuss,
And I don't
Come home
Angry

But tomorrow,
Tomorrow, I will

Willow Whispers

When cool winds blow
The willow whispers
Of the many secrets
Beneath her
Swaying skirt
Lightly touching
Silent lovers
Teasing them
With soft fronds

The willow whispers
And warm winds
Carry her secrets
To those with
Memories of love
Beneath her
Dancing shadows
To those who know
Her lonesome wail

Winning Hand

Been dealt a winning hand
Leaving for the promised land
Don't know when I'll be coming back
Can't turn this offer down, already packed

Going for a fresh new start
Come hold me close
Don't hold me back
Got to get on the straight and narrow

Clutching a royal flush in my hand
Leaving for the promised land
Be a fool to fold the deck
Promise to someday come back

Got to leave but not forever
Come hold me close
Don't hold me back
Though it hurts me to the marrow

Word Flow

Words wrestle each other
Tumbling as they fall from busy mouths
Some leap out covered in spittle
Vile, vulgar and frothing with spite
Needing time to cool off

Other words meekly escape
Exiting slowly, covered and hooded
Barely wanting to be heard
Afraid to cause pain
As though crossing traffic in fear
Cautiously glancing both ways

There are words of wisdom however
That hold, us spellbound
Looking down on us as children
Through omniscient eyes
Smiling benevolently as they wrap
Meaning around us, like a security blanket

Some words melt us with tenderness
Caressing the listener, and warming the soul
Sowing seeds of kindness,
Spreading roots that cling to us tightly
Developing long tendrils
Sometimes reaching to, forever…

Working Man's Hands

I want a pair of
Workingman's hands
Thick calloused palms
Sun-dried sausage fingers
Cut scarred tattoos
To the wrist
The kind of hands
My father earned
From decades of
Hard work and play

I want a pair of
Workingman's hands
Knuckles swollen and split
Dirt buried deep fingernails
With black and blue moons
Pinched by metal and wood
Never heard of manicures
Smell of diesel and oil

I want a pair of
Workingman's hands
That grip like bear traps
Shake firm with dignity and pride
Do what they mean
And mean what they do hands
Strong fingers that point out wrongs
And point on high

I want a pair of
Workingman's hands
Kind of hands that hold you back
With unbearable strength
Yet hold a newborn
With such tenderness

The kind of hands
My father owned

You Are Not A God

Let them go
All of them
Deliver yourself
Of self loathing and
Anguished rejection
Burdens which, own you
Heavy baggage not
Worth carting
A lifetime nor a day
Not a minute to waste
Liberate your spirit
Alight!
Alight!

Unload oppressions
That shackle
Your mind and heart
Burdens hobbling back
Or bend knee
You're not Atlas
You are not a God!
Refuse to carry
The world of pain
Contorting your face
Release the agony
Vexing your soul
Be firm stand erect
Alight!
Alight!

Youth vs. Wisdom

Torn and bruised flesh
Revealing
Buckle-shaped redness
Rising in welts
Minutely bleeding
On legs and back
One squarely
On cheek
Just below
Swollen eye
Black, blue,
Green and purple
Colored bruises
On arms, hands
Face, neck
And shoulders
Defiant reminders
Of my revolt
Against authority
Smart –mouthed
Over-zealous youth
Verses
Experienced
Hardened veteran
A perpetual combat
Between
Battered loser
And triumphant victor
An endless
Battle of wills
With no savior
At the bell

Zenith

Her face is sallow
Revealing bone through thinnest skin
She walks without purpose
Like a sloth at the zoo

Remembering how radiant she once was
Brings tears of sadness and frustration
Why would she want to kill herself this way?
"I'm high on life!" she used to say

She threw away her vitality and beauty
Her excuses died off long ago
Sadly, glimpses of her former self
Are seen only on the zenith of her latest high

About the Author

Manuel Nava Leal is an Author and Poet who has been involved in theatre for over thirty years as a director, actor, set designer, lighting and sound technician and just a few years ago added Playwright to his list of accomplishments.

Manuel has written short stories, prose and poetry since childhood and recalls creating and reciting stories early in life. He remembers at times entertaining close friends along with his sisters, with stories of love and adventure as well as tales of the paranormal and the supernatural. Together he and his sisters would perform before white cotton sheets hung on the line to dry. He writes often of those times growing up in the Rio Grande Valley in Southeast Texas, and specifically of Harlingen his place of birth and later on of his adopted city of Houston.

Manuel's passion is the short story, he has successfully converted several into theatrical productions and recently produced his fifth entitled "Even the Sun Cried," at Talento Bilingue de Houston.

Manuel is continually writing and is consistently inspired by life's subtleties, grandeur and mysteries.

Beautiful Heart, A Collection of Romantic Poetry by Manuel Nava Leal

Over time a person will fall in love. At that time, one feels a great emotional impact on their lives and may be at a loss for words.

Beautiful Heart is a wonderful collection of love poems to help express how one feels during this time of euphoria. Share these poems with the one you love.

Available at: CreativeHousePress.com

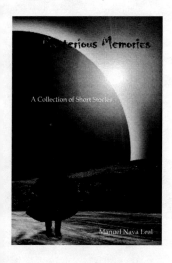

Mysterious Memories is a collection of short stories that leaves one to wonder if it is fiction or non-fiction.

Manuel writes with such honesty and accuracy that it takes the reader on a mysterious ride through time, space and reality.

Mysterious Memories is the second book by the talented playwright and author Manuel Nava Leal, available through Creative House International Press, Inc.. Please visit their web site at: **CreativeHousePress.com**